Pinch Me, I'm Breathing.

*A collection about life, love,
and holding your damn shit together.*

G.M. ELINOR

Dear Reader,

Writing evokes the most complicated yet entirely cathartic emotions in me. Above all, it reminds me to be grateful to anyone who takes time to sit with me in the rawness, the harshness, the beauty, the pain, and the healing. Thank you for that. Thank you for allowing me to feel and be felt. I hope these words can help you find some peace in knowing you are never alone, and that even in the darkest of moments, you can find light.

For anyone who has ever felt lost,
I hope these pages feel like home.

And to my Nell, thank you
for showing me what it means to be loved.

Contents

Here

You're not there yet, love.
But you're here.
And isn't that something?
Isn't that something
worth fighting for?

It Doesn't Last Forever

It doesn't last forever, you know. None of it.
You're going to hurt and cry
and you're going to feel all of the things that
will make you want to leave this life behind.
And you're going to believe that it will last forever.
No matter what they say.
But forever is a hell of a long time
and if you give yourself that time, I promise you
that this will end.
Life is an unpredictable mess of a thing
and you - you are an unpredictable mess of a thing.
But that's what makes you strong enough to take it on.
And you are stronger than you will ever know.

It Isn't All That You Are

Whatever it is that's taking over your mind
right now,
it isn't all that you are.
I don't care what it is or what has happened
to make you feel like anything less than
absolutely everything that matters.
It isn't all that you are, love.

It isn't all that you are.

You Are Not Broken

You are not broken.
You are not damaged beyond repair.
Maybe you're missing so many pieces that
you're not sure how you'll ever feel complete again.
And maybe it feels
as though this world has given up on you
because you just can't seem to find your place.
But listen when I say
that this world needs you around to make it whole.
And everything is out there waiting for you
to find your way home.

Inside Your Head

Don't become so introspective that
you start to lose your perspective.
There's more to you than what goes on
inside your head, love.
There's more to life than this.

Don't Dive Deep if You Can't Breathe Easy

Maybe some people just aren't meant to stay.
They drift in and out of our lives with the tide and
glide upon waves of emotion,
constantly crashing and coasting,
and swimming in every direction
except towards home.
Yet still you remain as the rip pulls you under
and suffocates your senses
until you get washed up on shore.
So tell me, love,
where is the glory in loving so much that you feel
like you're drowning?
Where is the glory in falling
so hard you forget where to land?
Listen: let them come, and let them go,
but don't you stop keeping your head above water.
Don't dive deep if you can't breathe easy.
And don't you dare sink for anyone, love.
Where is the glory in that?

Just Taking a Second

Sometimes you're going to get stuck.
It doesn't matter how far you've come
or how many demons you've exorcised along the way.
There are some ghosts that will always come back to haunt you.
But you can be haunted without getting hurt and
feelings can pass without knocking you down,
and you don't have to let your heart break to know
that it's still beating.
Getting stuck doesn't mean that you've gone backwards, love.
You're just taking a second to find your stride again.

Let it Out

I can see it in people - the pain.
I can see the past
that makes you so protective of your heart.
But you have to stay open, love.
You have to embrace this world for all that it is
or you'll never experience all that it can be.
All that you can be. All that you already are.
Please don't shut yourself off from possibility because
you're so terrified of ambiguity
that you've simply prepared yourself to fail.
There's more to you, love. So much more.
Let it out, and then let it in.

The Hard Part

Some people come into your life to stay.
I know that it's hard to believe.
I know that it's hard to place any faith in it at all.
But I promise you that it's true.
And sometimes you'll find them in the strangest of places or
meet them in the least obvious of ways. But once you do, you'll realise
that they just aren't going anywhere. No matter how hard you push.
And you'll push, oh I know that you'll push.
Pushing people away is the easiest thing in the world;
it's letting them stay that's the hard part.
But please, when you find one of these people, dig deep
and find the courage to know your worth.
Find the strength to be vulnerable and know that not everyone will leave.
Because you don't have to be alone. You've never really been alone at all.

Mo Chara

I hope life hasn't lent you a learned futility in loving.
For I have never met a soul with such capacity to heal.

Wounds

It will always stay with you, love.
I wish I could tell you that this pain will leave you
and that time heals all wounds in spite of it all.
I wish I could tell you that you can forgive and forget and that
coming to terms with it will mean that you can come to terms with
who you are now. With who you never became.
With who you never thought you would be.
I wish I could tell you that moving on means leaving it all behind
and that it never rears its ugly head again to get inside yours.
And I wish I could tell you that you could turn back time, love.
Oh how I wish I could tell you that.
But the truth is, you don't need any of it. You don't need to blow
out the candles or wish upon a star to get your life back.
You *are* the light, love.
And, my God, you shine brighter than any star that I have ever seen.
You radiate hope, love, determination, and the sheer damn
fucking grit that's brought you this far and helped you to make
your way through it all.
It will always stay with you, love.
But maybe who you've become now is the person you were
always meant to be. And maybe some wounds never
completely heal, so that we can let a little more light out
and a little more love in.

Someday

Someday you'll wake up and smile. And you'll wonder
how you ever felt any other way.
Your ghosts will lose their charm and you'll move on so fast
that the past won't know how to catch up with you anymore.
And it might take years, love. It might seem like it's taking forever
until suddenly it's not.
Until, someday, you wake up and smile. And wonder
how you ever felt any other way.

Hold On, Love

I don't think that you're too far gone
to find your way back.
It only seems that way
because somehow
all of the lights have gone out.
And I know you feel like this is the last time;
the worst time.
The time that's different to all of the times
that came before.
But it's not.
You've been here and survived and
the darkness will lift just the same.
Hold on, love.
If you keep your eyes set
on that spot
where the sun used to be,
I promise you it will rise once again.

Brace Yourself

The thing about this life
is that we can't predict what happens next.
And too much consideration often
leads to hesitation
that leaves us paralysed by fear.
It's okay to brace yourself for breaking, love.
But don't let it stop you from running
towards the things that make you feel whole.

Chasing Fire

We batten down the hatches in the face of rejection
and yet still chase our feelings like we're chasing fire.
Get too close and you'll get burned, they say.
But we get close anyway. We love, anyway.

And sometimes, we love so much that the whole damn thing
goes up in flames right before our eyes.
But sometimes, we love just enough.
And that fire becomes the only thing we've ever wanted.
The only person we've ever wanted.
To keep us warm, even when our blood runs cold;
to hold us, even when we say we don't want to be held.
To console us, even when we say we're strong enough
to do it all alone.

And to love us, even when we batten down the hatches
for fear that we're not worth much loving at all.
Get too close and you'll get burned, they say.
But we get close anyway.

We love, anyway.

Too Much

My love, don't ever let yourself feel
like you're "too much".
Don't change for anyone.
Don't shrink yourself to fit
inside of their ideals.

Some people just aren't ready for you yet.

Entirely Human

When you've built yourself back up it's terrifying to
embrace anything that could tear you down.
It's hard to let hope in and let fear go.
But when you finally find it,
when you finally find that space within yourself
that allows you to love truly and live freely.
Don't you dare run from it.
Don't you dare freeze in the face of everything that's possible.
Don't you dare settle for anything less than everything that makes you
so entirely human.
When you finally find it; stay.

Suddenly, You Were Here

Suddenly, you were here.
Just like that.
You walked right into this storm I call my soul
and painted me the brightest rainbow
in a world of black and grey.
And although I am not easy to hold,
I have found myself held.
And although I am not easy put at ease,
I have found myself at peace.
I found you when I didn't even know
that I was looking. Or what I was looking for.
And suddenly, you were here.
Just like that.

You Can Decide

You don't have to wait for people to change, you know.
You can decide. You can decide who's worth holding out
hope for and who isn't very worthwhile at all.
It's the very best in you that wants to find the best in them
but not everyone can turn over a new leaf. Not if this world
has already clipped the stem that breathes life into their souls
and dragged them right up from the root.
It's hard to save a heart that's already rotting at the core,
and it's not your job to bring them back, love.
Sometimes they're already too far gone.

Breathing Underwater

They expect you to play by the rules
when no-one ever told you where to draw the line.
When no-one ever told you that sometimes
loving means leaving
and that by merely living you could lose it all.
And I'm not sure how we learned
how to breathe underwater
in a world where mermaids don't exist.
Or how we manage to fly away inside our own
minds without ever sprouting wings.
But I don't think anyone has ever done much growing
by toeing the line.
So don't you worry too much about staying in that box
they've built to keep you out, love.
There's more to you than what they tell you to be.
There's so much more to you than that.

Leave

Here's the thing about some people;
they're never going to let you in.
And it doesn't matter how hard you push or don't push,
how much of yourself you give or don't give,
or how many times you walk away
only to come running back once more.
None of that matters, love.
You can't "figure someone out" if they simply don't
have anything to share.
You can't dive beyond the surface if it's barely 2 feet deep.
And you can't open a door that isn't there, love.
You can't change a person and it's sure as hell not okay
to let them change you in the breaking of you.
Leave.

Two Hearts, Two Humans

You didn't love her enough to leave her, but you
loved yourself enough to keep hurting her.
And that's what makes you the weaker of the two.
Two hearts, two humans,
just trying to survive
in the world that seems to have forgotten
to teach us how to love.
And when she left you feigned surprise
as if you thought this long time coming
would never come at all.
And maybe you were right. Somewhat.
Maybe she wasn't closing the door on you, love.
Maybe she was simply shutting out the noise.

Fly Free

I truly believe that some souls are just made for one another.
And if they do ever cross paths, what an incredible gift that is.
Don't you dare ignore that warmth in your heart, love.
Don't shy from letting yourself fly free.
Don't shrink your feelings to fit into society's best regards.
Don't... listen
to anyone other than the people who matter most.
Because if you do cross paths,
and two days turns into two weeks
and two weeks feels like two months,
and - hell - two years feels like it's more inevitable
than at all debatable.
Don't you dare ignore that warmth in your heart, love.
Shrink not. Stand tall. Fly free.

Pinch Me, I'm Breathing

You taught me how much I could love,
how hard I could hurt,
and why the struggle of such
contradiction is called living.

Memories Don't Fade as Fast as People

I walked past the telephone box beside your house today.
Except it isn't there anymore. Just like we aren't there anymore.
But memories don't fade as fast as people. And heartache
and heartbreak aren't always the same.
You said you loved me
in the same breath that you told me you wanted to die.
Held me close when you felt you could conquer the world
and then pushed me away
when you felt that this world had finally conquered you.
Made me keep secrets that anchored me to your pain
until finally you let me go free.
Until you made me go free,
for I'd never have left you of my own accord.
Sometimes the worst of wars bring us the best of peace
and the people we love become people we have to walk away
from - or be walked away from - so they can find their way.
But that telephone box will ring in my ears until the end of my days,
to remind me that we were once there
and you were once here
and a heart doesn't have to break to still ache
for what was.

Lights Out

I miss you. I miss you and
I feel it in the darkness more than ever.
But the lights are out and I don't
want you anymore.
And isn't that the strangest feeling
of them all?

Ashes

Ashes to ashes, dust to dust, and a lustful love
that can't decide whether to grow or fade away.
How many more times can we start over?
When does goodbye finally mean forever
and not "for later"?
Maybe we're in love but I'm not sure that
we know how to love each other.
And I can't keep putting out the fires
when we keep going up in flames.

She Is Not Yours

She is not yours. She is a wild one,
so you've tightened your grip.
But you cannot trap the one who cannot be caught
and you cannot tame the one who cannot be tamed.
And you cannot love her if you cannot love all of her wild ways
and her down days, and the pieces of her that make you lose your footing
because she knows how to hold her ground.
She is not yours, and if you cannot love her you must leave her.
Let her go.

Don't

Don't tell her you can defeat her demons,
if you can barely recognise your own.

It Takes Guts

It's the hardest thing to let someone go
before they've even started walking.
It takes guts, you know.
It takes guts to break your heart now
to stop both of you breaking later.
And it doesn't hurt any less just because you saw it coming.
It almost hurts more because you're left wishing
you didn't look for it at all.

Dust and Broken Hearts

We're all running around this world just trying
to find a reason to exist.
Racing from one moment to the next until
finally we stumble upon the one person
who stops us in our tracks.
And that's when we either stop to breathe or race on
leaving only dust and broken hearts in our wake.
Maybe it's okay to let someone make you happy, love.
Maybe it doesn't have to be so damn hard.
Life isn't passing you by; the truth is
you just haven't stopped running yet.

Sleepwalking

I'm tired of closing my eyes
whilst already asleep
walking blindfolded in this world of the living.

Don't Be Afraid of the Shadows

There's a peacefulness in moonlight that is nowhere to
be found in the light of day.
A stillness that lends itself to a comfortable pause
rather than a hasty hush
amidst the noise.
You see, when you learn how to
shine bright in the dark,
you'll never lose sight of the things that matter most.
You won't yearn for the spotlight
when you glow from the inside.
And you'll see more of yourself with your eyes shut
than your reflection could ever truly convey.
Don't be afraid of the shadows, love.
They can be your solace in the worst of storms.

It Will Get Better

It will get better, love.
However bad it is, it will get better.
But it might not be for always,
and you have to understand
that is the price we pay for living.
It might not be for always,
but it's more than enough for now.

Merely Human

Be careful with your heart, with your words, with your trust.
People often amaze me with their compassion and
their ability to be so much more than human.
But merely human is what we are, all the same.
I still wish for you to stay blind to the eye of the cynic
but I ask you to expect a little less than everything
just in case.
Feelings can be so easily hurt,
words so unfathomably misunderstood,
and trust so quickly and forever broken in the fallout of it all.

You're Beautiful

Don't ignore the warning signs, love.
No matter how much you want to understand people,
sometimes they just can't be understood.
Don't wait until it's too late
to walk out that door without leaving a part of yourself behind.
Don't stand for anything less than what you deserve just
because he's made you feel so completely undeserving.
You're worth more than this, love.
You're beautiful.
And some people, well, the only reason they come into your
life is to show you that you've been walking in the wrong direction.
So that the universe can steer you back
to where you're meant to be.
Don't ignore the warning signs, love.
Please.

Fear of Falling

You'd pick me right up off the ground like I was weightless,
in spite of everything that weighed me down.
And I'd scream at you to let me go, whilst holding on
for fear of falling too damn far.
That was us, love.
You'd say you loved me as I ran away
shouting "don't leave me"
and somehow even when it ended we'd always make
our way back to where it first began.
Until one day, I ran so far I lost my breath,
and you realised you couldn't love me back to life again.
It's hard to keep chasing someone who doesn't even know
that they keep leaving. And I'm sorry, love.
I'm sorry that I ever ran from you at all.

Tomorrow

Keep it together until tomorrow.
And the next tomorrow, and the
tomorrow after that.
The break will come, love.
The chaos will end.
And you will continue to heal.

Isolation

You wish that someone could understand,
but they won't,
they can't.
The only one who can ever get right inside
your head is you,
and you're stuck there.

Bled Dry

When we were both broken our wounds bled us dry
and we ended before we'd ever had a chance to begin.

And now you're back but you've stopped bleeding out
and I've stopped tearing myself up inside.

Have we healed now, love?
Is it real?

Rock, Paper, Rain

I tried to be your rock.
But when the pain rained down
you covered me in paper,
and I forgot how to breathe.

Free Yourself

I know it's scary. It's scary to move on.
But you have to free yourself from it all.
You need to know that letting go doesn't mean giving up;
it isn't a sign of weakness
and it doesn't make you any less of a person.
In fact, it makes you a stronger person on the other side of it all.
Not every situation can be controlled,
not every emotion can be anticipated,
and that's okay.
Because that's just life, love.
And life isn't meant to be a storybook with each chapter leading
seamlessly onto the next.
The outcome isn't meant to be predetermined
and the happy ever after doesn't always turn out as you expect.
But that's the thrill of the ride.
That's what makes it equally exhilarating and terrifying
at the very same time.
Don't live in fear of what comes next, love.
Embrace it,
because who knows what it may be.

Thoughts Before Sleeping

Don't rest easy in his arms for too long, love.
You don't belong there if it doesn't feel like home.

We'll Find Your Car, I'll Find My Mind

You told me you lost your car
after I told you I'd lost my mind
before either of us had even said hello.
And here we are still searching
for the things we think we need
to keep us sane,
whilst not quite understanding
the necessity of standing still.
Wait for a moment.
Breathe.
And when you say goodbye,
say it with the hesitance of knowing
what it is you left behind.
Come back in time with me, love.
We'll find your car, I'll find my mind,
and we can say hello.

Your Heart Is Not a Home

Your heart is not a home
for every lost soul that comes your way.
I know how much you feel,
I know how much you care.
But there is only so much love to spare
in every beat it takes for you to stay alive.

More

Don't spend all of your life "becoming more"
at the expense of appreciating
who you are right now.

Intoxicated

A drink that lasts mere moments
because you can't handle more of it and
I can't handle more of you.
A hug that's both a prelude and a conclude,
and a precursor to the distance in between.
A smile that asks a question I can't answer
and a sobriety not learned from the pint sat steady
in your hand.
A heavy heart leaning upon the defense of debatable
suggestion in the face of possible rejection,
because you know it just can't take another hit.
Fear. Pain. Loss. Hurt. Hope. A whole bunch of feeling
wrapped up in the conversation you thought we didn't have.
But you just didn't hear it, love.
It's hard to hear your heart beat
when you've almost forgotten
that you need to breathe to stay alive.

25;26

I suppose I never quite knew what to do about you.
You never stayed
and yet you never left for very long.
And now that you've been and gone
for the 25th time,
that arbitrary number doesn't seem to matter
so much anymore.
You don't seem to matter so much anymore.
But I'll see you on the other side of this;
when the clock strikes
one too many times
and the number 26 rolls around.
When you remember what it feels like to be lonely,
and I forget what it felt like to be left.

Growth

You don't need to be perfectly whole to heal.
But you need to know what parts of you are broken
so that you don't cut others with your edges
when you're hurting

Censored

So many people talk these days, but they never really listen.
And I miss that.
I miss real conversations about our futures and our passions
and the traumas that have made us who we are.
Instead, we censor ourselves to protect ourselves,
from each other.
And what a gut-wrenching tragedy that is.

Pause

Everyone is killing time
without ever noticing
the beauty in the moments it stands still.

The Beauty in the Balance

All of this is temporary, love.
These feelings, these moments, this... living.
You will heal and you will hurt and you will laugh and cry
and - hell - we're all going to fucking die anyway.
All of this will pass and time will rarely move at your pace,
but that's okay as long as you keep moving.
Because the beauty is found in the balance, love.
The spaces in between the lines.
The dots we join to make sense of our feelings
and the pages we turn when we need to start over again.
And you **can** start over again.
This life can't beat you for as long as you keep breathing.

Moments

It's only when the storm passes that
you finally stop holding your breath.
And yet we still keep searching
for the very moments
that will take our breath away.

The Abyss

I fell straight into the abyss before I realised
that I had lost my grip at all.
And reality turned its back on me as quickly
as this fantasy had taken a hold.
But I want it back now, love.
I want the hum-drum of this daily life and the
boredom of the most basic of endeavours,
and the freedom of living
within my own means.
I want it back now, love;
whatever it takes and whatever it means.
I don't belong here anymore.
Take me home.

Bridges

I keep building bridges
but I can't meet you in the middle
when you keep cutting corners
before we're even halfway there.

You and I

You're never alone, love.
Because - you and I -
we're looking at this world from behind
the same broken windscreen.

Castles

We made castles out of beer mats and made jokes
out of the spirits we found behind the bar.
And I wish time could have stood still, love.
I wish you had been more in love with you
and I had been more in love with me
and we had been able to love each other in a way
that made more sense than this ever could have.
But just like the brightest of stars in the night,
you burned out long before you came my way.
And when I found you, you were already gone.

Your Way

You were never much of a talker, but that was just your way.
And your way always felt like the right way to me.
But I'm not sure which way is right anymore.
Because I don't like the silence when you're not here.

Soul Sight

There is an art to sharing enough of yourself to let someone in
and still keep enough of yourself intact.
But it's only when I think I've mastered it that I realise I've lost it.
That's what happens when someone gets inside your soul, love.
They take away pieces of you to keep and they very rarely
ever give them back.
And only you can decide if it's worth it.
But I have yet to encounter a soul who saw right inside of mine
and left me any worse off for truly being seen.

Breathe

Give it one more day, love.
One more minute, one more hour,
one more chance for things to change.
To get better, somehow.
Because they might.
Because they can.
Give it one more day, love.
One more chance to get outside
of the inside of your head
and maybe time will tell you
more than these hours ever could.
Because it might.
Because it can.
Give it one more day, love.
Breathe.

Just Wake Up

Just wake up.
Wake up and get dressed and go out for a damn walk
even if it kills you.
Maybe you won't feel better. But you'll feel something else,
at least for a moment.
Let that moment find you. Let it fuel you.
Breathe the air into your lungs as if you were taking your very last gasp.
And then remember that with every end comes a beginning,
with every today comes a tomorrow,
and with every down comes the up that makes it all feel worthwhile
again.
Just wake up.
Live.

Lost and Found

I know that you feel like you've lost me.
But I've been busy finding myself again
in the time that you've spent mourning
who I used to be.
And the thing is,
I'm just not the same anymore.
Time changes people; life changes people.
And sometimes in the search for all your broken pieces,
you find out who you are when you're whole.

Expectations

They tell me to lower my expectations of people.
To avoid disappointment. To protect myself from the world.
They tell me not everyone cares... not everyone has to care;
that the world can be a cold, dark, and miserable place.
As if I hadn't lived through it all,
seen and felt it all,
and come out the other side not one fucking bit intact.
So yes, they tell me to lower my expectations of people.
But instead, I raise them as far as they can go and challenge you
to meet them somewhere along the way.
Not everyone cares. Not everyone has to care.
But everyone **can.**

Show Up

Start by showing up for yourself,
and it'll get easier to show up for the people you love.

0101

It's the glass of water on the bedside locker.
It's the simple untangling of a curling wand cord.
It's the dress now folded far away from its dishevelment on the floor.
It's the broken light, now shining. It's the arms wrapped around me
as tightly when I wake as when I sleep.
It's the food in my belly, the warmth in my heart,
and the smile in my soul. It's this.
It's you. It's me. It's us.

The Break

There's always a break in it, love.
Even when it feels like you're drowning
you'll make your way back to the surface
to breathe.

Wait for the break.

Learning. Living. Still.

I am learning, still.
Learning that not everything that breaks is broken,
and not everything that aches will stop aching.
Learning that not everyone stays but not everyone leaves, either.
And not every heart you fall into will turn yours to stone.
I'm learning that sometimes physical pain can't be overcome
but mentally you have to find a way through.
And the reverse of that same regard also applies.
Learning that if you feel both parts of yourself crumble at once,
you must choose a side to bear the weight until you find your balance.
And you must choose a side, love,
choose a side to hold you up and don't you dare let this world
push you down.

I know it's hard to stay standing with a shoulder so burdened,
but I promise I am standing here with you.
For I am learning, I am living, still.

Release

Sometimes the tears just won't fall,
your cheeks stay dry and your stance stays stoic,
but you know inside your heart is bleeding all the same.
I guess that the worst of droughts don't just happen when nature goes off
course;
they happen to us too, when our world goes so far left of centre
that we're not sure where the way home is anymore.
But it won't last for long, love.
You'll find your release when you're ready to allow yourself to dwell
in those tears for just a little while.
And then you'll let the love around you soak them up so you can move on.
It won't last for long, love. Stay strong.

Trauma Lens

Have you ever noticed how often we normalise trauma?

We cherry-pick the "highlights" (albeit perhaps not the most appropriate term) and just skip the rest completely. I mean, I get it, I do. If your entire life has been a clusterfuck of chaos then how do you differentiate from one disaster to the next?

But it's so gut-wrenchingly sad when you really think about it.

We just do it. We pick one thing, because God forbid we talk about everything horrible that's ever happened in case anyone thinks we're feeling sorry for ourselves.

And then we put all of that pain, all of that sadness, and the weight of everything - on to one single thing. And when that one single thing explodes, we ask why everything has hit us all at once. When, in fact, it never stopped hitting us. We just stopped noticing.

It's time to notice, love. For if we always pick our battles, we might never win the war.

Free

Not everyone is going to understand you.
You have to make your peace with that.

It's the only true way to be free.

Seasons

I know you're scared, love.
Change never comes easy.
Those autumn leaves may be pretty to the eye but
they get trampled upon all the same.
People change as seasons do
and their hearts can warm you just as quickly
as their words can leave you frozen in time.
And I'm not sure if it's about giving up
or simply letting go.
Or maybe it's about moving on from the things
that have always kept you in one place
by realising it's just not where you're meant to be.
Either way, it's about knowing that you can't stay where you are.
And finding the strength to walk away from
anything or anyone
that doesn't make this life a little more worth living.

Recognise the Non-Essentials

Don't waste time on the opinions of people
who don't invest time in knowing you.

Playing with Fire

We fall in love with our demons,
and feign wonder,
when hell rises up at our feet.

Turn The World Off

I need to turn the world off for a minute.
I have lost my patience for these talking heads
sat upon fetal souls that know nothing of life.
And the tolerance I call a virtue is both waning
and washing me away.
I'm losing myself in the lives of other people.
Losing my compassion to the cynicism
I feel rise within myself in response
to their sheltered naivety.
I struggle to find the empathy to lend
towards shallow conversations about misguided ideations,
blanketed by societal expectations.
Still jumping recklessly but falling slowly
in the hope that somehow they'll miss the ground.
I need to turn the world off for a minute
before I lose myself in it.
I need to breathe.

Rebirth

I read that almost all of our cells get replaced every 7 years
and I've been counting down the time ever since.
The time it takes for a soul to reclaim itself,
a body to rebuild itself,
and a person to find their way home.

Someday

Someday all of this will be behind us
and we'll remember the start of us.
I'll see you there, love.
I'll see you then.

Deja Vu

I thought I was searching for the friendships I'd lost, but I realised perhaps it was myself that I was looking for all along.

As I've been piecing myself back together I've been trying to connect the dots along the way to find a path from there to here.

A map to trace who I was then to who I am now. A way to find the best inside the worst of people I lost along the way and bring them back into my life again.

But maybe it's only when we go looking for the remnants of the world that made us who we were that we realise they no longer fit into the world that best serves us now.

And it's sad. It's sad as hell when it hits you.

But some people are better held close as memories, than recurring moments that get stuck on repeat only to fuel the fire of regret.

And sometimes it takes a step back to see that you can't move forward with yesterday still slowing you down.

Perspective

Show me the worst of you
and I will still find
the very best of you
beneath it all.

Someday it's Going to Hit You

Someday it's just going to hit you out of nowhere.
You might be sitting in the car, walking to work. watching a show,
or just drifting off to sleep.
And it's going to hit you, just like that.
You're going to realise that your heart doesn't hurt
like it used to.
Your memories don't have the power they once had
over you.
Your shoulders are carrying less weight than ever before
and you can't recall the last time that
living felt... heavy.
Someday it's going to hit you out of nowhere.
You made it. You survived it.
You're still here.

Reclaim Your Future

When life itself
has become a threat,
reclaiming it becomes the
scariest thing in the world.

Love Her First

Love her first, before you fail her.
And damn, you'd better love her hard.
Because you will fail her.
Not because you don't love her.
Not because you hate her.
Not for any other reason than this one
unremarkable truth; you are human.
So love her first and love her hard
because not every love survives the fall.

Reflection

I needed to be there with you
to get to where I am now with me.

Reprieve

We scourge for dreams
within the seams of
tear-stained sheets
where we've barely slept,
but often wept
whilst waiting
to drift away.

All At Once

You hold me, and I let you.
You touch me, and I feel you.
You break me, and I heal you.
You love me, and I love you.
And I am with you and without you
all at once.

This Middle Part

You called it living;
I called it surviving.

But this middle part?
Damn, it's the scariest of them all.

Connection

I don't know how to let you in,
without pouring myself out.

Impact

Sometimes you just have to do things.
You just have to get up and go out and do something, anything,
to remind yourself that you're alive.
And you don't have to love it. You don't have to like it, even.
They say if a tree falls in the woods
it's questionable whether it makes a sound.
Don't you dare fall without making a sound, love.
So that if you do fall,
you'll go out with one hell of a fucking bang.

Stop Holding On to What's Hurting You

I thought that no-one stayed
because I was broken.
But the truth is that
I was holding on
to broken people.

Find Yourself First

Please don't lose yourself in love
before you find yourself in life.

Undone

There are words that can never be unsaid
and things that can never be undone.
And yet you are my undoing all the same.

Bones

There are 206 bones in the human body,
and yet not a single one has to break for us to shatter.

Look, Listen, Run

It's hard to work out which light means "go"
when you first learned to cross the road
without a hand to hold.
Trial and error. Green and red.
Look, listen, run. Don't get... dead.

I always ran from one side to the next.
Never anticipated the crash.
If you know what's coming you can't get crushed by it.
Or can you?

The ambulance would race past every now and then
and I'd wonder why it didn't just knock me down
along the way.
All good things come to those who wait, right?

I was 7 years old when I got tired of waiting for a good thing.
I was 7 years old when I realised that nothing put on hold goes very far.
I was 7 years old when I learned that crossing the road
doesn't always mean you'll get to the other side.

I was today years old when I stopped seeing red
because I learned how to trust in green.
And that it's okay to keep going
even when you're not sure where you'll end up.

Be Present

This is where you're at. And maybe it hurts.
Maybe it's shit.
Maybe it's downright unbearable at times.
But you need to sit in it, love.
You need to sit in it and take the time to map your way out of it;
as uncomfortable as that may be.
Because tomorrow will come when it comes
but this is where you're at.
Don't dwell for so long that you miss it.

I See You

Sometimes you just need someone to say they see you.
You just need someone to say that they see the pain, the fear, the loss, and all of the things you can't explain and perhaps they can't completely understand.

But they see you struggle and they see you here.
Still here. Still standing. Still you.
Sometimes that's all you need.
Sometimes it's everything you need and more.

I see you.

I Am With You

I am with you. I am with you when the pain engulfs your present
and you fall into the void of the space in between.
The space where you cannot seem to find yourself
amidst the noise of feeling.
The space where everything you knew becomes everything you are
and equally as if it's all you'll ever be.

I am with you here, now,
in the past and the present and the future that has yet to unfold.
And I am sorry, love.
I am sorry for every single thing that has hurt you so deep down inside
that tomorrow brings you fear rather than fortune.
I am sorry for every single day that you have felt alone in this world
when there are so many of us here to stand by your side.
I am sorry for the ways in which society has unfolded that force you to
hide
the beautiful bare bones of your being.

But I am with you. Here.
In this space. In the past. In the present. In the now.
And I will ask no more of you than to stay standing,
because I know you cannot unfeel all of this feeling.

Nostalgia

There are stories to be found in the faintest of memories
if you can just recall the feeling.

Growth

It's okay to outgrow people, you know.
Sometimes life takes you in a direction
that doesn't have a place on the map they look at anymore.
And I know you want to hold on.
I know the last thing you want to do is let go.
It's never easy to move on from the past,
especially when it's staring you right in the eye.
But it's better to leave with a smile and an open door,
than a wall of resentment
built from all of the doors that slammed shut.

The Noise

Maybe you're stuck right now.
Caught in a loop of repetitive days and nights
that seem to serve only to smother or silence you.
Because you've simply lost your voice amidst all of this damn noise.
The world is full of it now: noise.
Our heads are full of it now: noise.
So we try to drown it out, but sometimes drown ourselves out with it.
It's time to take control now, love.
It's time to turn down the noise outside and turn *your* volume up.
It's time to speak the words that come to mind late at night without the
presence of anyone who could possibly mind what they're made of.
What you're made of.
It's time to speak those words without concern
for who is on the receiving end.
Because you know that you've spoken your truth.
It's time now, love. It's time to truly speak,
whilst there are still those left fighting the noise so they can listen.

Stop Assuming

Stop assuming.
I know it's one of the toughest things to do
but that shit is going to consume you.
It's going to be a thorn in your side when you're simply trying
to love and be loved.
It's going to dig deeper every single time you draw upon your inner
trauma
instead of your inner sense,
to come to a conclusion.
A conclusion you came to in 5 seconds flat because your head bypassed
your heart
and convinced you what happened before, would happen again.
Or your self-doubts bypassed your logic and insecurity took over...
And convinced you that of course something was wrong,
because it was always going to go wrong, because you're broken.

Stop assuming.

You are better than the trauma that taunts you
and the doubts that prey upon you.
You are better than the what ifs
and the tears that stream as soon as you start to believe them.
You are better than a love you have to question every day
simply because you can't seem to get away from the pain you left behind.
You are better. Give yourself a chance to see that.
Please.

You Made it Here

You can be borne to broken people
and still be whole.
Don't let those who brought you here
dictate how you survive
the war they threw you into.
This is your time now.
Your life.
Your fight.
And although you can't undo what's happened to you,
you can trust yourself to move beyond it.
You can trust in your strength to endure life as you did
and still stay whole.
And I'm proud of you for that.
I am in awe of you for that.
You made it out, love.
You made it here.

Most People

I truly believe that most people are inherently good.
You'll always find a little goodness in someone,
hidden somewhere beneath the hurt
that stole their belief in healing

Loops That Lead to Nowhere

I think sometimes we invest so much of our hopes
into who we want someone to be,
that we become blinded to who they truly are.
And so, we get stuck in this loop of getting let down
by the promises made by those
who were never truly able to fulfill them;
because we made them feel like they could or they should,
which does nothing to serve anyone in the end.
They feel frustrated at best, inadequate at worst,
and we feel alone in realising the person we created
never existed at all.

Thanks for Sitting in the Fire With Me

Some people will never know what to make of you.
You'll intrigue them. You may even unnerve them.
And in time you will realise that you'll always be you
regardless of them.
And sometimes, that will be the reason you lose them.
Some people just aren't built for discomfort, you see.
They don't have it in them to sit in the middle of everything
that makes you fire,
without burning in the heat.
But there are others, love. And you'll find them.
You'll find people who will sit in your fire
and know when to put it out
or when to fan the flames and watch it rise.
Watch **you** rise.
You'll meet people who will know exactly what to make of you
because you know exactly what to make of them
and then, my love;
wherever you may be, you'll know you're home.

Remember

Your pain isn't linear.
Your healing won't be either.

Reminder

You're still you.
It's not your fault that they stopped loving you for that.

Life Moved On: We Stayed

I was completely confused by you when we first met.
Confused but intrigued in a way that made you feel
like someone worth knowing;
someone who made me feel worth knowing.
Someone who made me feel worthwhile.
Now I'm still here with all of my feelings
spurting out into sentences that I'm not sure make sense.
And you're still here with your way of making me feel heard
without one ounce of pretence.
And although we were never sure where we were going,
we somehow ended up exactly where we were meant to be.
Life moved on but we managed to stay;
and I'm still completely confused by you,
but I'm not sure I'd have it any other way.

Lessons

I have little left to give except the lessons
in all that I have lost.
And yet I still leave pieces of myself
in all that I have loved.

Blind

I want to do the right thing, whatever the right thing is.
But figuring that out is the hard part.
I want to opt out of this game where everyone is playing pretend
and telling me to follow the rules.
Why can't we just "be"?
Why must we "be" anything different at all?
Constant changing. Rearranging.
Never truly satisfied with having it all
because there is too much we deem worth having
and too little that we feel deserving of... deep down inside.
We surround ourselves with things to make life more bearable
instead of looking inside for what's making it so hard to breathe.
But you're suffocating yourself with all of this chaos
and you can't see it, love.
You've spent so long searching for brighter lights
that you've gone blind.

The World Moved On

I was there, and then I wasn't.
It felt as though time stood still
and yet I was losing it
in all of the spaces in between.
Battle scars, tired hearts, wounded souls,
and words that no longer made
the same sense
that they used to.
Everything changed and tried to
drag me with it,
but I stayed in that same place.
I stayed where I was safe,
and then the world moved on
without me.

It's Okay

It's tough when you want to protect people, I get that.
You lock all of the hurt and pain and all of this feeling inside yourself
so they don't have to feel it too. And that's okay, some of the time.
It's okay to want to do it all on your own. It's okay to want to be
on your own.

It's okay to share what you can and shoulder the weight you can carry.
It's okay to let people in without letting all of yourself out.
Sometimes by protecting them, you're also protecting yourself, and that's
okay too.

No-one can tell you the right way to get through this; there is no right
way to get through.

You just get through, and that's it.
And the people who are still there when you do,
are the people worth holding on to.

Somewhere

I like to believe that somewhere
in the universe of "what could have been",
there's another you and I.
Two people who have finally learned
how to hold hands
without breaking hearts.

Stop

Stop being who everyone else wants you to be.
It's exhausting. It's pointless.
And it's going to steer you so far away from yourself
that eventually you'll forget who you truly are.
Stop hiding the best parts of yourself in fear
of finding yourself ostracised by those who have yet to find themselves.
I want to know you. I want to know what drives you and what haunts you
and what lurks inside the very bones of you, love.
Let it all out. Let yourself be seen.
But don't let them make you light up
just because they're still afraid of the dark.

Hold Tight

You're flailing, and maybe it feels like you're falling.
But you don't need anyone to save you, love.
Just hold tight and I promise that you'll catch yourself
before you've even caught your breath.

Don't Push Me

I learned a long time ago that people leave.
If you're in my life
I probably already rehearsed your exit
before I let you through the door.
It says pull.
Don't push me.

Find Yourself First

Find someone who ties your shoelaces when your bones hurt
and holds your hand when your heart hurts.
Find someone who can pull you up
when you know you're further down than grounded.
But someone who also knows you can do that shit without them.
That part's important.
And listen, love, find yourself first.
Because it's hard as hell to find someone to connect with
when you're still trying to figure out what fucking frequency you're on.

You Can Choose

You can choose who to love.
You can walk away from anything
that doesn't feel like it's enough.
You can walk away from anyone
who doesn't make you feel like *you're* enough.

It might not seem like it now, when butterflies and anxiety
feel so interchangeable that you're unsure if you're in love
or just plain terrified of never being loved at all.
But you can choose.

You can choose to want more.
You can choose to love better.
To be loved... better.
Do it now.

He's Going to Come Back

He's going to come back. He's going to come back
again and again for as long as you keep letting him in.
But you must stop, love.
You can't keep wasting your years in tears that never stop falling.
In fear that stops you falling... too deeply, into something more.
This isn't it. This isn't how love is supposed to be.
Love isn't meant to harden you and turn your heart cold;
love should keep you warm and hold you near.
That feeling in your gut that turns your insides out - that isn't love - it's
fear.
And he's going to come back.
He's going to come back again and again
and you're going to doubt every single fucking thing,
but you must stop, love. You must not let fear win.

Never Settle

Don't be a work in progress for anyone but yourself, love.
Never settle for anything less
than being loved
for everything single fucking thing that you are.

Don't Come Knocking

I boxed you up and put you in the past where you belong.
I shut the door and said goodbye to hurt, regret, and fear.
So don't come knocking, love.
There's no room left for you here.

Leave Whilst You're Still You

If someone takes you and breaks you
when you're already broken,
it's time to pick up those pieces
and walk away whilst you're still intact.
Don't wait too long, love.
Leave whilst you're still you.

Feel Your Feelings

They say to forgive and forget,
but I'm here to tell you that it's okay to **feel**.

They Told Me About People Like You

They told me about people like you.
Steady. Solid. Happy. Grounded.
Funny. Passionate. Caring. Kind.
People who light up a room when they enter so that
all of the monsters hidden in dark corners disappear.
People who tell you everything or tell you nothing
without an ounce of deceit or dishonesty in between.
People who make you feel safe
like you've never felt before;
with two arms that open wide to let you in and wrap
around you so tightly they shut the whole world out.
They told me about people like you and I wondered if
they truly were real. And I wondered if any of them
would ever want me.
I don't wonder about that anymore.

Take Control

You can't change how you got here, love.
But you can take control of where you go
from where you are.

This Won't Go On Forever

Maybe you're there still. Right back where I started without an end in sight.

Unable to breathe anything but heaviness into your lungs with each hour that passes by.

And unsure of the days because they all seem to merge into one. One single solitary moment relived in every single day.

But I want you to know that this won't go on forever.

Someday you'll find your peace and this life won't feel so cold and desolate anymore. And the air you breathe will stop cremating you from the inside out.

Keep searching for a tomorrow that's better than this. You'll get there one day and you'll wonder how you ever made it through at all.

And you'll see that the strength within you is enough to overpower whatever it is that has broken you. That day will come, love. Don't give up when you're so close to finding all of those pieces of yourself that have got lost in time.

You can't reclaim the past,
but you can move into the future and rediscover who you are.

There Will Be People

There will be moments when it feels like this world
has swallowed you whole
and your dreams have abandoned you to the night.
And there will be hours when it feels like giving up is all that there is left
because you can't find anything worth fighting for.
But then, my love, there will be people.
There will be people who will build you up when this life tears you down.
People who will fill the silence with compassion
and turn despair into determination.
There will be moments, and they will try to break you, but there will
always be people to put you back together.

Printed in Great Britain
by Amazon

16941042R00077